SWU-NAP- 022

UNIFORMS OF RUSSIAN ARMY DURING THE NAPOLEONIC WAR VOL.17

UNDER THE REIGN OF ALEXANDER I
EMPEROR OF RUSSIA BETWEEN 1801 AND 1825
GUARDS CAVALRY: HUSSARS, LANCERS, COSSSACKS & OTHERS

From the Viskovatov's greatest work:
"Historical description of the clothing and
arms of the Russian Army"

English translation by Mark Conrad

SOLDIERSHOP PUBLISHING

AUTHOR

Aleksandr Vasilevich Viskovatov born 22 April (4 May New Style) 1804, died 27 February (11 March) 1858 in St. Petersburg, Russian military historian. He graduated from the 1st Cadet Corps and served in the artillery, the hydrographic depot of the Naval Ministry, and then in the Department of Military Educational Institutions. He mainly studied historical artifacts and the histories of military units. Viskovatov's greatest work was the Historical Description of the Clothing and Arms of the Russian Army.

PUBLISHING'S NOTE

NOTE ABOUT BOOK PRINTING BEFORE 1925

LICENSES COMMONS

ACKNOWLEDGEMENTS

A Special Thanks to NYPL and other institutions for their kindly permission to use some images of his archives, collections or books used in our book.

Title: **UNIFORMS OF RUSSIAN ARMY DURING THE NAPOLEONIC WAR VOL. 17**
The Guards Cavalry: Hussars, Lancers, Cossacks & Others
By A.V.Viskovatov. Serie edit by Luca S. Cristini. First edition by Soldiershop. March 2018
Cover & Art Design: Luca S. Cristini. Plates re-colorations by Anna Cristini.
ISBN code: 978-88-93273107
Published by Soldiershop publishing, via Padre Davide, 7 - 24050 Zanica (BG) ITALY. www.soldiershop.com

UNIFORMS
OF THE RUSSIAN ARMY
DURING THE NAPOLEONIC
WAR VOL. 17

UNDER THE REIGN OF ALEXANDER I EMPEROR OF
RUSSIA BETWEEN 1801 AND 1825

*

THE GUARDS CAVALRY: HUSSARS, LANCERS
COSSACKS & OTHERS

HISTORICAL DESCRIPTION OF THE CLOTHING AND ARMS OF THE RUSSIAN ARMY - A.V. VISKOVATOV

(First English translation by Mark Conrad)

Soldiershop is glad to presents the complete collection of the great job made by A.V. Viskovatov dedicated to the uniforms and weapons belonging to the Russian army during the Napoleonic period, until 1825. The time we considered corresponds to the reigns of two Tzars: Paul I, who reigned since 1769 until his murder on the 23rd of March 1801, and his son Aleksandr Pavlovič Romanov, that with the title of Alexander I, sat on the throne until the 1st December 1825.

Our reprint in based on the original 19th century volumes, to be precise the volumes from 7 to 9 are dedicated to the reign of Paul I; this first part is distributed on 7 volumes, having a numbering from 1 to 7. From number 10 to 18 of the original volumes, the second part is dedicated to the Russian troops under Alexander I. These still being worked on and they will be soon ready, distributed on twenty volumes approximately. Our new edition, the first ever published in English, both on paper and digital format, boasts a large number of color plates, many of them unpublished and coloured by our team of expert artists and scholars of uniformology. Each volume is based on 50/70 plates, always accompanied by the original translated text which describes the uniforms, the organization and the armament of the Russian army of the period.

In this book we present the Russian Guards cavalry regiments of the Napoleonic wars (2nd part).

A unique work in its genre, a must have in any respecting collection!

Aleksandr Vasilevich Viskovatov born 22 April (4 May New Style) 1804, died 27 February (11 March) 1858 in St. Petersburg, Russian military historian. He graduated from the 1st Cadet Corps and served in the artillery, the hydrographic depot of the Naval Ministry, and then in the Department of Military Educational Institutions.

He mainly studied historical artifacts and the histories of military units. Viskovatov's greatest work was the Historical Description of the Clothing and Arms of the Russian Army (Vols. 1-30, St. Petersburg, 1841-62; 2nd ed. Vols. 1-34, St. Petersburg - Novosibirsk - Leningrad, 1899-1948). This work is based on a great quantity of archival documents and contains four thousand colored illustrations.

Viskovatov was the author of Chronicles of the Russian Army (Books 1-20, St. Petersburg, 1834-42) and Chronicles of the Russian Imperial Army (Parts 1-7, St. Petersburg, 1852). He collected valuable material on the history of the Russian navy which went into A Short Overview of Russian Naval Campaigns and General Voyages to the End of the XVII Century (St. Petersburg, 1864; 2nd edition Moscow, 1946). Together with A.I. Mikhailovskii-Danilevskii he helped prepare and create the Military Gallery in the Winter Palace.

He wrote the historical military inscriptions for the walls of the Hall of St. George in the Great Palace of the Kremlin. (From the article in the Soviet Military Encyclopedia.)

◀ *The Russian Zar Alexander 1st in a portrait by Stepan Semyonovich Shchukin. Now in Stockolm museum.*

CONTENTS

*

RUSSIAN ARMY- GUARDS CAVALRY

CHANGES IN THE UNIFORMS AND EQUIPMENT OF GUARDS CAVALRY FROM 1801 TO 1825.

XXXVI. GUARDS HUSSARS.
[Gvardeiskie gusary.]

11 May 1801 – The L.-Gds. Hussar Regiment was ordered to have dark-blue **dolmans** and red **pelisses**, **sabertaches**, and **saddlecloths**. However, in all regards the previous patterns were continued, as were the existing uniform clothing, accouterments, weapons, and horse furniture (Illus. 2054, 2055, and 2056) [106].

21 July 1801 – Generals and field and company-grade officers of the troops in the St.-Petersburg garrison, including the L.-Gds. Hurssar Regiment, were ordered, when wearing undress coats, to wear **hats** of the same pattern as that introduced at this time for other regiments of Guards cavalry [107].

29 December 1802 – Confirmation was given to a new **table of uniforms, accouterments, and weapons** for the L.-Gds. Hussar Regiment, based on which, as well as on a supplementary directive of **20 August 1803**, this regiment was prescribed all the uniforms, accouterments, weaponry, and horse furniture as Army Hussar regiments (Illus. 2057, 2058, 2059, and 2060), while colors remained as before, except for saddlecloths [*valtrapy*] which, instead of the red prescribed on 11 May 1801, were ordered to be the same dark blue as the dolmans, and with a new pattern of piped embroidery, namely: yellow with two rows of thin yellow cord and two of red, sewn on with crenelations [*gorodki*] and small rings. Also, the eagles on the corners were replaced with monograms of yellow cloth trimmed, as were the crowns, with thin red cord. Cord of the same color, but thicker, was prescribed to be sewn around the edge of the entire saddlecloth (Illus. 2058). Sabertaches remained red, as before, with yellow monogram, crown, and edge, but trimmed with thin black cord that was not previously prescribed (Illus. 2058). Officers—who from this time no longer had the decorative leather harness (*sarsam*) on their horses—were given cartridge pouches and new pattern sabertaches and saddlecloths. The cartridge pouch, of black leather, was covered in very dark-blue velvet, mounted in gilded bronze fittings, and had on the cover a two-headed eagle surrounded by rays, also of the same kind of bronze (Illus. 2061 and 2062). The pouch belt, of red morocco, was trimmed on the outer side with gold galloon mixed with very dark-blue silk, and decorated with a gold laurel wreath enclosing the HIGHEST monogram. All its fittings were metal, that is to say: prickers, chain, buckle, slide, and endpiece, gilded and with the same decorative tracing as on the cartridge pouch's mountings (Illus. 2061 and 2062). The sabertache, also of red morocco, was trimmed on its upper surface with red cloth, as before, on which was rich gold embroidery with the HIGHEST monogram under a crown, and, and with a palm branch of green silk (Illus. 2061 and 2062). The saddlecloth, of dark-blue cloth, was trimmed around the edges with wide toothed gold galloon and thin cord. At the ends, of embroidered gold, silver, and silk, were: the monogram of the EMPEROR, a crown, and a stand of arms (Illus. 2061 and 2062). The *undress coat* [*vitse-mundir*], with which was worn the standard cavalry hat and saber, was the same as in other Hussar regiments, i.e. dark green, with red lining and skit turnbacks, but it had a red collar and cuffs with gold tracery (the same color as the buttons), and on the right shoulder a gold aiguilette (Illus. 2063) [108].

In 1804 – The **hat** prescribed for the officer's undress coat was ordered to be of the same pattern as that established at this time for the whole Army, i.e. with a buttonhole loop of narrow galloon and not embroidered, and with a high plume (Illlus. 2064) [109].

4 April 1805 – The collar on the **cloaks** for field and company-grade officers, previously gray with red piping, were replaced with ones completely red [110].

1 October 1806 – The **warm coats** [*fufaiki*], or short fur coats [*polushubki*], prescribed for lower ranks were withdrawn [111].

2 December 1806 - Lower ranks lost their **queues** and **side curls** and were ordered to cut their hair short under a comb, while Generals and officers were allowed to proceed in this regard according to their own wishes [112].

17 September 1807 – When wearing the undress coat, generals and field and company-grade officers were ordered to have the previous gold **aiguilette** on the right shoulder, and on the left shoulder—an **epaulette**. This was to be of the same pattern as that established at this time for the rest of the Guards regiments (Illus. 2064) [113].

12 November 1808 – Officers, when wearing the undress coat, were ordered to have dark-green *chakchiry* **pants** [114].

27 March 1809 – These same persons, when in the undress coat, were ordered to have two **epaulettes**, and consequently the aiguilette was taken away [115].

25 April 1809 – All combatant ranks in the regiment, instead of the white *chakchiry* **pants**, were ordered to have dark-blue ones, the same color as the dolman, decorated (in front, on the side seams, and behind) with galloon and flat thin cord or braid—yellow for lower ranks (Illus. 2056 and 2066) and gold for officers (Illus. 2067 and 2068) [116]. Along with this change these same personnel were given new **shakos** in all respects the same as for Guards infantry, but with a difference in the color of the pompon, which for privates was yellow surrounding a red center [117]. Privates had a white hair plume, non-commissioned officers—white with black and orange at the top, trumpeters—red, staff trumpeters—red with black and orange at the top, and officers—all white (Illus. 2065 and 2067) [118].

8 June 1809 - The plumage on **generals' hats** (when wearing the undress coat) was discontinued and the former pattern of buttonhole was replaced with a new one made of four thick, twisted cords, of which the two middle ones were intertwined with each other in the form of a plait [119].

20 November 1809 – Instead of dark-blue **dolmans**, the L.-Gds. Hussar Regiment was ordered to have red ones with dark-blue collar and cuffs, and on the **barrel sash**, or girdle, the slides were to be dark blue instead of red (Illus. 2065 and 2067) [120]. In this same year officers were given **frock coats** [*sertuki*] of dark-green cloth with red lining, a red collar, dark-green cuffs piped red, and the same gold decorative tracery on the collar and cuffs as on the undress coat (Illus. 2069) [121].

10 February 1810 – The **shako cords** of private Hussars and trumpeters, instead of being yellow with red, were ordered to be just yellow. However, for non-commissioned officers and staff-trumpeters they were white with black and orange. Officers' shako cords remained silver with black and orange. Along with this, all combatant ranks were given **plumes** of a new design, thinner than before and wider at the top than at the bottom, as was introduced throughout the whole Light cavalry beginning in 1812 (Illus. 2070) [122].

16 June 1810 – Carbines and **pistols** for the Guards Hussars were ordered to be made according to newly confirmed patterns. Both of these were of indentical caliber with infantry muskets (seven lines, measured in English inches [i.e. 0.7 inches - M.C.]) [123]. In this same year the **plumes** on generals' and officers' hats were shortened, canes were abolished, and officers' shako cords became completely silver without any admixture of black and orange silk [124].

17 January 1811 – **Shako cords** for non-commissioned officers and staff-trumpeters were ordered to be as for privates—yellow—and only their tassels would be in three colors: white, black, and orange [125].

23 September 1811 – The L.-Gds. Hussar Regiment was given new **forage caps** of the pattern introduced at this time throughout the Guards and Army, colored dark blue with a red band [126].

In the beginning of 1812 – The L.-Gds. Hussar Regiment was given new **shakos**, lower than before, with a pronounced expansion or widening toward the top and indented at the sides. Also, the **collars** of pelisses, dolmans, cloaks, and officers' undress and frock coats were ordered to be lower than before, without a diagonal opening in front and instead closed with small hooks (Illus. 2071 and 2072) [127].

10 December 1812 – Carbines and **bandoleers** are withdrawn from the L.-Gds. Hussar Regiment, and subsequently the only remaining firearms were pistols and the sixteen musketoons (for the flankers) in each squadron [128].

6 April 1814 – Officers' **undress coats** were ordered to be singlebreasted with nine buttons, and as before with red collar and cuffs and red piping down the front opening and below to the turnbacks (Illus. 2073). **Frock coats** were to be without the gold decoration, with round cuffs instead of the previous pointed ones, and with white lining instead of red (Illus. 2073) [129].

20 May 1814 – The gray **riding trousers** for campaign wear that officers had since 1802, with buttons and leather reinforcements, were replaced by new ones of the previous gray color but without buttons and leather. The new trousers had wide stripes and piping the same color as the collar on the undress coat, i.e. red (Illus. 2073) [130].

19 August 1814 – Similar **riding trousers**, except with leather reinforcements, were given to lower ranks [131].

15 September 1814 – The regiment was issued 1120 **carbines** and—in place of the musketoons—112 **rifles** [*shtutsera*], which were ordered to be worn on white **bandoleers** with brass buckles, prongs, and endpieces [132]. In the same year of 1814, officers were ordered to have **hats** with white ribbon around the cockade, later changed to silver, and to no longer use the **panther skins** [*barsy*] authorized for parades since the time of EMPEROR PAUL I [133].

[Note by M.C.: An advertisement in *Sanktpeterburgskiya Vedomosti*, 20 January 1814, No. 7, announced that "Furrier Karl Steinberg... now in Sadovaya Street... makes fur coats of various sorts, women's coats, muffs, gloves, etc., and also **tiger skins lined with silver for Hussar Officers**."]

25 February 1816 – All combatant ranks were ordered to have five rows of **buttons**, instead of three, on dolmans and pelisses, with one row being of large size and four small. There was a new design for the gold tracery on **pants**; **Boots** and **shakos** became higher than before, with the latter having a flat top instead of indented (Illus. 2074 and 2075). Lower ranks were to sewn narrow yellow tape around the thin cord and cuffs of the pelisse and dolman (Illus. 2076 and 2077). Officers were to have **pelisses** and **dolmans** without fringes, and the cord on these was to be placed in rows side by side without any space in between. The fur on the pelisse was to be beaver, and the **galloon** on the swordbelt straps and sabertache, as well as the small tassels on boots—gold (Illus. 2077 and 2078) [134].

13 March 1816 - When assigning **remounts** to the L.-Gds. Hussar Regiment, it was ordered that any color horse be selected except light bay, Isabellas [i.e. palominos], spotted, sorrel or light-brown Tatar breeds, light chestnuts tending to yellow, and pigeon grays or ash colors [135].

16 April 1817 – The L.-Gds. Hussar Regiment's previous red morocco **cartridge pouches**, with similar belts, were replaced with black leather ones with the same round badge as for the L.-Gds. Dragoon and L.-Gds. Horse-Jäger Regiments, a pistol ramrod on a white deerskin strap, and a whitened crossbelt, also of deerskin, which privates were ordered to wear not over the right shoulder as had been done previously, but over the left shoulder (Illus. 2078). Along with this, the regiment was given new **sabers** with a black grip and iron hilt, arched guards, and solid scabbards without cutouts (Illus. 2078) [136].

6 May 1817 – **Trumpeters** were ordered to have dark-blue swallows' nests on the sleeves of their dolmans and pelisses, and sewn-on tape—yellow with thin red stripes (Illus. 2078) [137].

19 September 1817 – Shako **chinscales**, for lower ranks as well as officers, were ordered to be covex instead of flat [138].

10 August 1818 – The rings and edging on the collars and cuffs of officers' **undress coats** were ordered to not be of thin cord and lace, as previously, but embroidered [*vyshitye*] (Illus. 2079) [139].

16 February 1819 – When on campaign or in camp, the regiment was ordered to have **covers** on shakos and plumes, identical to those established at this time for Guards Dragoons and Horse Jägers [140].

18 February 1819 – All combatant ranks in the regiment were given new **shakos**, higher than before, wrapped with red cloth instead of black; with yellow woolen tape for lower ranks and gold galloon for officers, on the sides and around the upper and lower edges (Illus. 2080) [141].

28 February 1819 – Field and company-grade officers were given new **sabers** of the same pattern as established at this time for the Life-Guards Dragoons and Life-Guards Horse Jägers (Illus. 2080) [142].

In March of 1823 - With the introduction of the rule that Guards Cavalry regiments have **horses** of one color, the Life-Guards Hussar Regiment was ordered to have grays [144].

19 February 1824 – The *Life-Guards Grodno Hussar Regiment* [*Leib-Gvardii Grodnenskii Gusarskii polk*], newly formed in Warsaw, was ordered to have: olive-colored [*olivkovago sveta*] dolmans and pelisses with white trim; fur on the pelisses to be black astrakhan; *chakchiry* pants, shakos, and sabertaches raspberry with white; white pompons; white waistbelts [*poyasa*], with raspberry slides (Illus. 2081, 2082, 2083, and 2084); in the shield of the eagle on the shako was the image of a Lithuanian horseman; wide stripes and piping on the riding trousers raspberry. Saddlecloths were prescribed to be raspberry with white trim and thin white and raspberry cord (Illus. 2085a), but it was permitted to use—and indeed such were used—fleece saddlecloths of black astrakhan. The latter was trimmed around with raspberry cloth, with an insert of thin white cord, and had white monograms and white crowns with thin raspberry cord. Both the monograms and the crowns were cut out of raspberry cloth, sewn onto the fleece (Illus. 2085b). Officers had uniform clothing of the same colors as lower ranks, but with silver appointments. The waistbelt, cartridge pouch, and galloon on the pouch crossbelt were silver (Illus. 2086 and 2087), while the undress coat had a dark-green collar and cuffs on which was raspberry piping, and raspberry cuffs and skirt turnbacks (Illus. 2088 and 2089b). In other regards, all patterns, accouterments, arms, and horse furniture in this regiment corresponded to those used in the Life-Guards Hussar Regiment, but horses were bays [*kariya*] [146].

29 March 1825 - For combatant lower ranks, for faultless service, there were established **stripes** [*nashivki*] to be sewn on the left sleeve: for 10 years service - one, for 15 years - two, for 20 years - three; one over the other, all of yellow tape (Illus. 2090) [147].

18 August 1825 – The hair plumes on shakos in Guards Hussar regiments were abolished, and in their place it was ordered to have round **pompons**: for lower ranks—of yellow wool, and for officers—silver (Illus. 2090) [148].

Russland.

Flankeur
vom Rgt. Jelissawetgrad.

Husar
vom Rgt. Pawlograd.

Russische Husaren.
1813.

Seit Ende des Jahres 1812 sollten sämtliche russischen Kavallerie-Regimenter 6 Feld- und 1 Depot-Eskadron stark sein. 16 Mann jeder Eskadron wurden als Flankeure mit Karabinern ausgerüstet. Das erste Glied trug Lanzen. An Stelle der engen ungarischen Beinkleider wurden im Felde graue Ueberknöpfhosen getragen. Die meisten gleichzeitigen Darstellungen zeigen nur wenige Seitenknöpfe. Merkwürdig erscheint, dass auf fast allen gleichzeitigen Abbildungen russischen Militärs die Czakos auch im Felde mit Behängen erscheinen. Darstellungen russischer Czakos in Ueberzügen kommen nur äusserst selten vor. Der Czakostutz

XXXVII. GUARDS LANCERS.
[Gvardeiskie ulany.]

12 December 1809 – The *Life-Guards Lancer Regiment*, formed from half of HIS HIGHNESS THE TSESAREVICH CONSTANTINE PAVLOVICH'S Lancer Regiment, was prescribed all the uniforms, accouterments, and weaponry, as well as horse furniture, as it had before this reorganization, except the *shapka* headdresses had a two-headed eagle of the standard guards pattern. Saddlecloths had two rows of yellow tape [*bason*] (gold galloon for officers) along red cloth trim. Buttons, badges, and other metal appointments on uniform clothing were copper [*krasnaya med'*, or "red brass"] instead of the previous yellow brass (Illus. 2091, 2092, 2093, 2094, and 2095) [149].

23 September 1811 – A new pattern of **forage cap** was confirmed for the Life-Guards Lancer Regiment, identical to that established at this time for the whole Army, very dark blue [*temnosinii*] in color with a red band [150].

20 November 1811 – **Pennons** on the lances in the L.-Gds. Lancer Regiment were ordered to be of nankeen [*kitaichatye*] instead of taffeta [*taftyanyi*], without any change in color, i.e. white with red [151].

In the beginning of 1812 – In the Life-Guards Lancer Regiment **collars** on jackets and greatcoats were ordered to be lower than before and closed with small hooks. Thin **plumes** were issued that were wider at the top than at the bottom. **Sabers** with iron guards at the hilt were issued in all-iron scabbards (Illus. 2096) [152].

17 December 1812 – **Pompons** on lower ranks' headdresses were ordered to be yellow instead of red, while officers' cords and tassels [*kitish-vitishi*] were all silver without the previously used admixture of black and orange silk (Illus. 2096) [153].

20 May 1814 – The **riding trousers** for officers in use since 1803, with leather reinforcement and buttons, were replaced with new ones, gray as before but without leather and buttons, and with wide red stripes and piping (Illus. 2097) [154].

25 July 1814- The L.-Gds. Lancer Regiment was ordered to remake their **uniform** according to the pattern used by Polish Lancer regiments, i.e. with short skirts sewn together, with ten buttons, with the side of the skirt having a wide turnback of red cloth in the shape of a triangle, and in between these turnbacks, in two places, were cutout patches of dark-blue cloth like pocket flaps, with red cloth piping. The same piping ran down the center from the top or waist buttons to the bottom buttons (Illus. 2097 and 2098) [155].

19 August 1814 – Lower ranks of the L.-Gds. Lancer Regiment were given a new pattern of **riding trousers**, similar to those established on 20 May for officers, except with leather on the lower leg (Illus. 2098) [156].

11 December 1815 – Officers of the L.-Gds. Lancer Regiment were given **frock coats** like those established at this time for Army Lancer regiments, but with a red collar and dark-blue cuffs piped red [157].

16 December 1816 – Trumpeters were ordered to have gray **horses**, and other ranks to have dark colors [*temnaya sherst'*] [158].

13 March 1816 - When assigning **remounts** to the L.-Gds. Lancer Regiment, it was ordered that any color horse be selected except light bays, Isabellas, spotted, sorrel or light-brown Tatar breeds, light chestnuts tending to yellow, and pigeon grays or ash colors [159].

6 May 1817 – **Trumpeters** of the L.-Gds. Lancer Regiment, apart from their current sewn-on tape on wings and sleeves, were ordered to have additional tape on their lapels, along all seams, and along the edges of the skirt turnbacks (Illus. 2099) [160].

19 September 1817 – Lower ranks in the regiment were ordered to have convex **chinscales** on the headdress instead of flat. Officers, though, had chains as before [161].

2 March 1818 – *The Grand Duke and Tsesarevich Constantine Pavlovich's L.-Gds. Lancer Regiment*, newly established in Warsaw, was prescribed all the same uniform and other items—except for headdresses and lance pennons—as for the L.-Gds. Lancer Regiment, but with white distinctions instead of yellow. Yellow headdresses were issued, of the pattern used by regiments in the Lithuanian Lancer Division, with a Lithuanian horseman on the eagle's shield. Lance pennons were red with yellow, while sewn-on tape on the uniforms of lower ranks was yellow with thin red stripes, as in the L.-Gds. Lancer Regiment (Illus. 2100, 2101, 2102, and 2103) [162].

18 April 1818 – New **headdresses** were confirmed for the L.-Gds. Lancer Regiment, following the pattern used by THE GRAND DUKE AND TSESAREVICH CONSTANTINE PAVLOVICH'S L.-Gds. Lancer Regiment, but red instead of yellow, with the previous plate, and with yellow distinctions instead of white (Illus. 2104 and 2105) [163].

16 February 1819 - When on campaign or in camp, the L.-Gds. Lancer Regiment was ordered to have **covers** on the headdress, identical to those established at this time for Army Lancer regiments [164].

28 February 1819 – Field and company-grade officers were given new **sabers**, of the same pattern as received at this time by the L.-Gds. Dragoons, L.-Gds. Horse Jägers, and L.-Gds. Hussars (Illus. 2106) [165].

In 1820 – Tape [*bason*] on **trumpeters' coats** in both regiments began to be sewn on closer together and around the entire collar (Illus. 2107) [166].

21 December 1821 – Officers of both Guards Lancer regiments were ordered to have their **horses** "Anglicized" [*anglizirovannye*] [i.e. nicked, meaning cutting the tendon at the root of a cropped tail to make it stand up – M.C.] [167].

In 1822 – Lower ranks of THE GRAND DUKE AND TSESAREVICH CONSTANTINE PAVLOVICH'S L.-Gds. Lancer Regiment were given yellow **epaulettes** instead of white, in accordance with the color of the coat's sewn-on tape (Illus. 2106 and 2107) [168].

In 1823 - With the introduction of the rule that Guards Cavalry regiments have **horses** of one color, the Life-Guards Lancer Regiment was ordered to have sorrels [*ryzhie*], and THE TSESAREVICH'S L.-Gds. Lancer Regiment—chestnuts [*gnedye*] [169].

29 March 1825 - For combatant lower ranks, for faultless service, there were established **stripes** to be sewn on the left sleeve: for 10 years service - one, for 15 years - two, for 20 years - three; one over the other, all of yellow tape [170].

18 August 1825 – Both Guards Lancer regiments were ordered to have round **pompons** on their headdresses instead of pyramidal, keeping the previous colors, i.e. yellow in the L.-Gds. Lancer Regiments and white in THE GRAND DUKE AND TSESAREVICH CONSTANTINE PAVLOVICH'S L.-Gds. Lancer Regiment. For officers in both regiments, pompons were silver (Illus. 2107 and 2108) [171].

Russland.

Ulan.   Offizier.   Ulan.

Ulanen-Regiment Grossfürst Thronfolger.
1806.

▲ *The Russian lancers. Plates by Knotel*

XXXVIII. GUARDS COSSACKS.

[Gvardeiskie kazaki.]

14 March 1801 – Along with its previous uniform clothing, accouterments, and arms, the **L.-Gds. Cossack Regiment** was ordered to have jackets [*kurtky*] or half-caftans [*polukaftan'ya*] and *chekmen* coats or caftans [*kaftany*] with standing collars, open in front (Illus. 2109). For their collars and cuffs, officers were given two rows of the same silver embroidery that up to this time they only had along the coat's front opening, and when on parade or in formation they were directed to wear standard officers' sashes [*sharfy*] and cartridge pouches [*lyadunki*]. The sashes were tied over the everyday white girdles [*kushaki*], while the pouches were of black leather on a crossbelt trimmed with silver galloon, and they had a silver badge, chains, prickers, buckle, prong, endpiece, and rings—all in silver (Illus. 2110). The lid of the pouch was covered with black velvet, and around it was set a silver frame with similarly silver rays in the corners, and in the center it had a silver eight-pointed star with a two-headed eagle (Illus. 2111) [172].

14 and 15 April 1809 –New **uniform clothing** was confirmed for the L.-Gds. Cossack Regiment:

a) *For privates* – dark-blue caftan coat, scarlet half-caftan, both with a standing collar, slit cuffs, and sewn-on tracery colored red with yellow; dark-blue *sharavary* pants; epaulettes of the pattern for Guards lancers with tinned brass buttons [*mednyya, vyluzhennyya pugovitsy*]; white girdle, headdress of black astrakhan, with a red top and white hair plume [*sultan*] with black and orange at its root; mixed yellow and red cap lines and a black chinstrap, fastened on the right side with a tin button; gray greatcoat with a red tab on the collar and a red strap on the left shoulder (Illus. 2112).

b) *For non-commissioned officers* – as for privates but with the addition of silver galloon on the collar and cuffs; white cap lines with a mix of black and orange; white plume with black and orange hairs at the top (Illus. 2113).

c) *For trumpeters* – the same as for non-commissioned officers with the addition of dark-blue wings and sewn-on guards tape: on the chest, wings, sleeves, and all seams. Also, instead of white plumes, they had red (Illus. 2114).

d) *For company-grade officers* – caftan, half-caftan, and sharavary pants, of the same colors and patterns as described above—the first with the embroidered tracery already in use; silver epaulettes of the pattern for company-grade officers in the rest of the Guards; plume—as for privates; silver cap lines with an admixture of black and orange silk; the previous cartridge pouch except the black velvet replaced by dark blue, and on the star the eagle was gold instead of the previous silver; crossbelt for the pouch, covered with the same velvet, with silver galloon over its entire width, and with likewise silver badge, chains, and prickers (Illus. 2115 and 2116).

e) *For field-grade officers* – as for company-grade officers except epaulettes had a fringe (Illus. 2115).

f) *For generals* – as for all officers, but with silver generals' embroidery along the edges of the collar and cuffs and on the pocket flaps of the caftan coat; epaulettes with thick twisted cord for a fringe; silver cap lines; a plume [*cheleng*] of white feathers, with black and yellow feathers towards the bottom, as on the shakos and headdresses of Hussar generals (Illus. 2117) [173].

11 September 1811 – The L.-Gds. Cossack Regiment was given **forage caps** of the same pattern as introduced at this time throughout the Army, but in red with a dark-blue band and piping. Lower ranks additionally had the squadron number on the band, in thin yellow cord (Illus. 2118) [174].

In the beginning of 1812 – **Collars** on caftans, half-caftans, and greatcoats were ordered to be lower than before and closed by small hooks. For lower ranks the collars had the straight sewn-on lace prescribed for the entire Guard, and for officers—the previous silver embroidery. Also, the **cap cords** for privates became completely yellow, and for non-commissioned officers—yellow with multicolored tassels and knots. For officers the cords were completely silver (Illus. 2118 and 2119) [175].

25 April 1813 – The ***L.-Gds. Black Sea Sotnia***, attached to the L.-Gds. Cossack Regiment and also known as the *L.-Gds. Black Sea Squadron*, was ordered to keep all its existing uniform clothing. In color and pattern, the uniform was like the clothing for the other Cossacks, i.e. Don, of this regiment, but on the half-caftan as well as the caftan, the squadron added to the normal sleeves two more, thrown back. These were red for the half-caftan and dark blue for the caftan. There was another difference in that collars and cuffs in Don squadrons were of red and dark-blue cloth (corresponding to the color of the half-caftan and caftan), trumpeters' wings were dark blue, and shabracks and saddle pads for all ranks were red with white trim, while in the Black Sea Sotnia collars and cuffs were black (of plissé for lower ranks and velvet for officers), with white piping; wings were red; shabracks dark blue; and saddle pads red with yellow tape for trim (Illus. 2120 and 2121) [176].

20 November 1815 – Field and company-grade officers of all squadrons in the L.-Gds. Cossack Regiment, in place of their previous embroidery, were ordered to have silver **buttonhole loops** [*petlitsy*] on collars and cuffs (Illus. 2122, 2123, and 2124). Privates and non-commissioned officers [*ryadovye i zauryadniki*] were given new cartridge pouches, of the same pattern as used by Guards Lancers (Illus. 2125) [177].

Пикетъ Уральскихъ Козаковъ.
Piquet des Kosaques d'Oural.

11 February 1816 – Instead of black plissé and velvet **collars**, the L.-Gds. Black Sea Squadron was ordered to have these of plain cloth: red for half-caftans and dark blue for caftans. Also, lower ranks were given yellow headdress cords instead of white (Illus. 2123) [178].

3 April 1816 – In the L.-Gds. Black Sea Squadron, it was ordered that the yellow woolen tape on lower ranks' **shabracks** and **saddle pads** be replaced with trim in white lace, following the example of the other squadrons [179].

16 February 1819 – The L.-Gds. Cossack Regiment was ordered to have **covers** on headdresses and plumes, closed with small hooks and overlapping on the left side, similar to the shako covers introduced as this time in Dragoon, Hussar, and Horse-Jäger regiments (Illus. 2126) [180].

28 February 1819 – Officers of the L.-Gds. Cossack Regiment were ordered to have **sabers** of the pattern introduced at this time for officers of the rest of the Guards Light Cavalry, i.e. with a gilt hilt (Illus. 2126) [181].

In 1820 – **Trumpeters' tape** sewn onto half-caftans and caftans began to applied more closely together and around the whole collar (Illus. 2127) [182].

18 August 1825 – The regiment was given round **pompons** instead of hair plumes. For lower ranks these were of yellow wool, and for officers—silver (Illus. 2128 and 2129) [183].

XXXIX. GUARDS GENDARMES.
[Gvardeiskie zhandarmy.]

27 December 1815 – The newly established *Life-Guards Gendarme Half-Squadron* was ordered to have the uniforms prescribed for the Gendarme Regiment on 30 August of this year, but with sewn-on yellow Guards tape for lower ranks, yellow epaulettes instead of shoulder straps, and a yellow aiguilette instead of white (Illus. 2130). Officers, in addition to silver buttonhole loops, had embroidered silver edging to the collar, cuff flaps, and cuffs (Illus. 2131 and 2132). Saddle cloths were prescribed to also be as for the Gendarme Regiment, but with two rows of yellow tape (silver galloon for officers), and yellow crowns and monograms for lower ranks, trimmed round with thin red cord (Illus. 2130 and 2131). Accouterments and arms were as for the Guards Dragoons [184].

3 April 1816 – All combatant lower ranks of the half-squadron were ordered to wear blue [*svetlosinii*] **pants** for everyday use, matching the color of the coat. They were to put on white pants only for parades, and while on campaign have gray riding trousers with blue stripes and red piping (Illus. 2133) [185].

24 June 1816 – The same personnel were ordered to have slit **cuffs** without flaps, with two silver buttonhole loops for officers (Illus. 2133) [186].

15 May 1817 – They were also ordered, when in formation or in parades, to be in **gloves** with gauntlet cuffs, after the manner of Cuirassiers (Illus. 2134) [187].

In 1820 - **Trumpeters' tape** began to be sewn on more closely together and around the whole collar (Illus. 2135) [188].

29 March 1825 - For combatant lower ranks, for faultless service, there were established **stripes** to be sewn on the left sleeve: for 10 years service - one, for 15 years - two, for 20 years - three; one over the other, all of yellow tape [189].

XXXIX. GUARDS TRAIN.
[Gvardeiskii furshtat.]

6 February 1817 – Clothing, accouterments, and weaponry were confirmed for lower ranks of **train battalions** in the Guards Corps, all according to what was approved on 9 may 1819 for Army Train personnel and already described above, except that on the shako was a Guards pattern badge (Illus. 2136) [190]. Officers were given uniforms like those of Army Train officers, but with the Guards badge on the shako and embroidered silver buttonhole loops on the collar and cuffs (Illus. 2137) [191].

25 October 1819 – In order to distinguish between the different Guards Train battalions, lower ranks of the 1st Battalion were ordered to have **shoulder straps** with red piping, the 2nd Battalion—with white, the 3rd—with green, and the 4th—with no piping [192]. This same distinction was also adopted for the piping around the upper edge of the **forage cap** [193].

15 March 1822 – Guards Train officers were given **frock coats**, identical to those prescribed for officers of the Army Train [194].

29 March 1825 - For combatant lower ranks, for faultless service, there were established **stripes** to be sewn on the left sleeve: for 10 years service - one, for 15 years - two, for 20 years - three; one over the other, all of yellow tape [195].

NOTES

(106) Report by the Commissariat Office to the Government Military Collegium, 11 May 1801; memorandum to this Office from the L.-Gds. Hussar Regiment, 23 May 1801, No 2136.

(107) PSZ Vol. XLIV, pg. 72, No 19,950; pg. 61, No 20,169, and pg. 49, No 20,186, and statements by contemporaries.

(108) Highest confirmed table of uniforms, accouterments, and weapons for the L.-Gds. Hussar Regiment, 29 December 1802; drawings located in the SOVEREIGN EMPEROR'S Own Library, catalogued under No 246; various uniforms and other contemporary items preserved up to the present time, and statements by contemporaries.

(109) Statements by contemporaries.

(110) Proposal by the General-Intendant to the Commissariat Office, 4 April 1805.

(111) From the files of the War Ministry's Commissariat Department.

(112) HIGHEST Order announced to the Military Collegium by the Minister for Military Land Forces, 2 December 1806.

(113) From the files of the War Ministry's Commissariat Department.

(114) Ditto.

(115) PSZ Vol. XLIV, pg. 13, No 23,548.

(116) Ibid., pg. 14 No 23,609.

(117) Ibid.

(118) From the files of the War Ministry's Commissariat Department.

(119) PSZ Vol. XXX, pg. 1006, No 23,695.

(120) From the files of the War Ministry's Commissariat Department.

(121) Ditto.

(122) Ditto.

(123) PSZ Vol. XXXI, pg. 215, No 24,263.

(124) Statements by contemporaries.

(125) From the files of the War Ministry's Commissariat Department, and statements by contemporaries.

(126) Ditto.

(127) Ditto.

(128) PSZ Vol. XXXII, pg. 454, No 25,262.

(129) From the files of the War Ministry's Commissariat Department, and statements by contemporaries.

(130) Ditto.

(131) Ditto.

(132) Ditto.

(133) Ditto.

(134) Ditto, and contemporary drawings and uniforms.

(135) PSZ Vol. XXXIII, pg. 543, No 26,192.

(136) From the files of the War Ministry's Commissariat Department, contemporary drawings; oral statements.

(137) Ditto.

(138) Ditto.

(139) Ditto.

(140) PSZ Vol. XLIV, pg. 101, No 27,618.

(141) From the files of the War Ministry's Commissariat Department; contemporary drawings and actual shakos.

(142) Order of the Chief of H.I.M. Main Staff, 28 February 1819, No 15, and actual sabers.

(143) From the files of the War Ministry's Commissariat Department; statements by contemporaries, and actual items.

(144) Ditto.

(145) Ditto.

(146) Ditto.

(147) PSZ Vol. XL, pg. 188, No 30,309.

(148) From the files of the War Ministry's Commissariat Department.

(149) Highest confirmed table of uniforms, accouterments, and weapons for the L.-Gds. Lancer Regiment; uniforms, *czapka* headdresses, and other contemporary items preserved up to the present time, and statements by contemporaries.

(150) From the files of the War Ministry's Commissariat Department.

(151) PSZ Vol. XLIV, pg. 57, No 24,883.

(152) From the files of the War Ministry's Commissariat Department; actual items from that time, preserved at this Department and in various Arsenals; contemporary portraits, drawings, and statements by contemporaries.

(153) From the files of the War Ministry's Commissariat Department.

(154) Ditto.

(156) From the files of the War Ministry's Commissariat Department, and PSZ Vol. XLIV, pg. 120, No 25,644.

(157) PSZ Vol. XLIV, pg. 102, No 26,018.

(158) From the files of the War Ministry's Commissariat Department.

(159) PSZ Vol. XXXIII, pg. 543, No 26,192.

(160) From the files of the War Ministry's Commissariat Department, and statements by contemporaries.

(161) From the files of this Department.

(162) PSZ Vol. XLIV, pg. 104, No 27,298.

(163) From the files of the War Ministry's Commissariat Department; statements by contemporaries, and actual items.

(164) PSZ Vol. XLIV, pg. 101, No 27,681.

(165) Order by the Chief of H.I.M. Main Staff, 28 February 1819, No 15, and actual sabers.

(166) From the files of the War Ministry's Commissariat Department.

(167) PSZ Vol. XXXVIII, pg. 679, No 29,241.

(168) From the files of the War Ministry's Commissariat Department.

(169) Ditto.

(170) PSZ Vol. XL, pg. 188, No 30,309.

(171) From the files of the War Ministry's Commissariat Department.

(172) Information extracted from the files of the War Ministry's Commissariat Department; drawings located in the SOVEREIGN EMPEROR's Own Library, catalogued under No 246, and actual pouches preserved up to the present time.

(173) PSZ Vol. XLIV, pg. 14, No 23,581.

(174) From the files of the War Ministry's Commissariat Department.

(175) Statements by contemporaries and information extracted from the files of the War Ministry's Commissariat Dep.

(176) Highest Ukase addressed to the Acting Minister of War, 25 April 1813, in the city of Dresden, and information extracted from the files of the.

(177) PSZ Vol. XLIV, pg. 102, No 26,002, and information extracted from the files of the War Ministry's Commissariat Department.

(178) Highest confirmed pattern uniforms for the L.-Gds. Black Sea Squadron, 11 February 1816.

(179) Highest order announced to the War Minister, 3 April 1816, No 195.

(180) PSZ Vol. XLIV, pg. 102, No 27,681.

(181) Order of the Chief of H.I.M. Main Staff, 28 February 1819, No 15, and actual sabers.

(182) From the files of the War Ministry's Commissariat Department.

(183) Ditto.

(184) PSZ Vol. XXXIII, pg. 419, No 26,049; Highest confirmed table of uniforms, accouterments, and weapons for the L.-Gds. Gendarme, 24 June 1816, and model examples located in the War Ministry's Commissariat Department.

(185) Highest order announced to the Duty General of H.I.M. Main Staff, 3 April 1816, No 193.

(186) The table cited in Note 184.

(187) Order of the Chief of H.I.M. Main Staff, 15 May 1817, No 45.

(188) From the files of the War Ministry's Commissariat Department.

(189) PSZ Vol. XL, pg. 188, No 30,309.

(190) Highest confirmed pattern uniforms preserved in the War Ministry's Commissariat Department.

(191) Contemporary uniform coats and statements by contemporaries.

(192) PSZ Vol. XLIV, pg. 139, No 28,429.

(193) From the files of the War Ministry's Commissariat Department.

(194) PSZ Vol. XLIV, pg. 139, No 28, 969.

(195) Ibid., Vol. XL, pg. 188, No. 30,309.

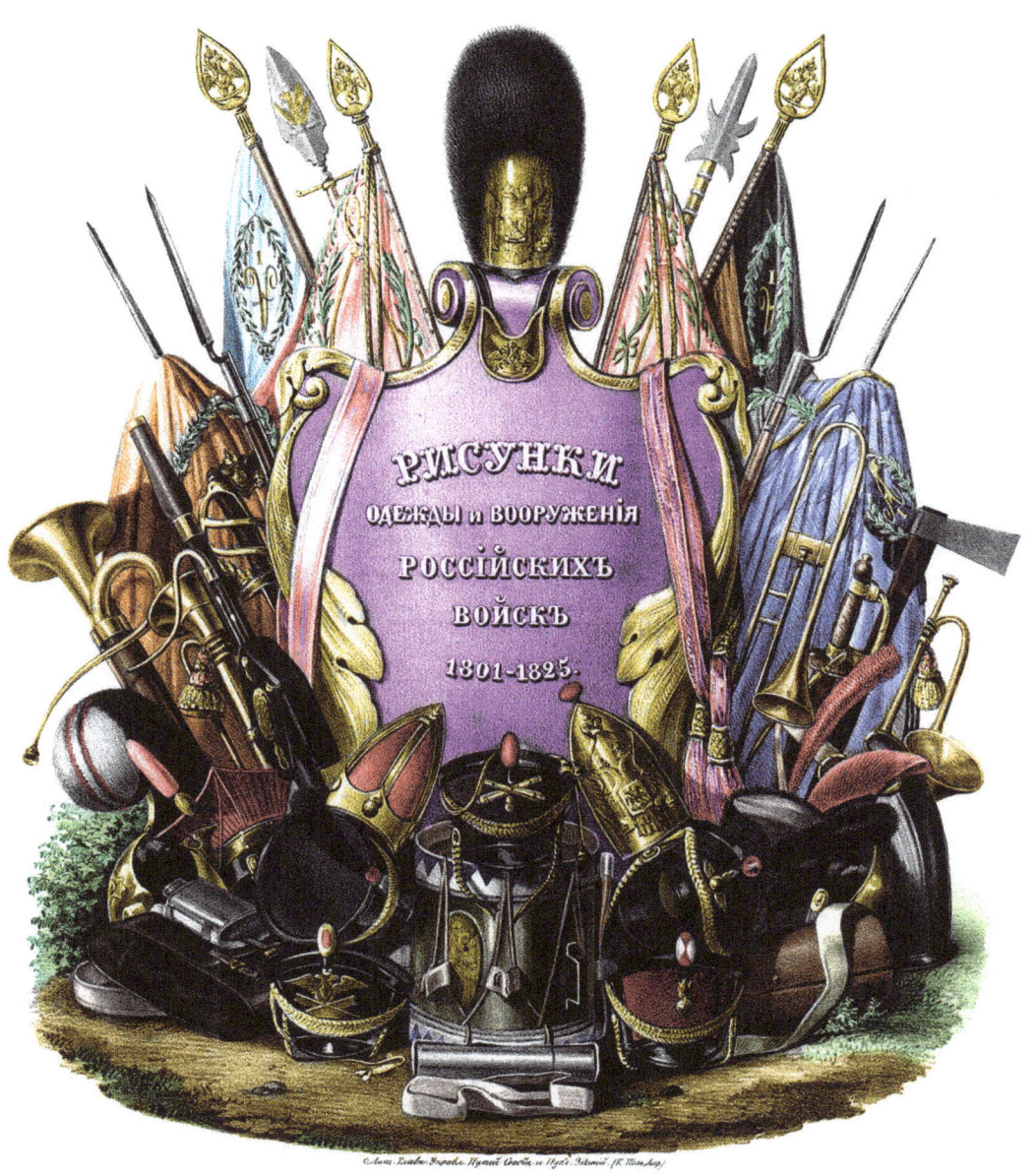

РИСУНКИ
ОДЕЖДЫ и ВООРУЖЕНІЯ
РОССІЙСКИХЪ
ВОЙСКЪ
1801-1825.

PLATES LIST OF ILLUSTRATIONS

2097. Company-Grade Officer. L.-Gds. Lancer Regiment, 1814-1818.

2098. Non-Commissioned Officer and Private. L.-Gds. Lancer Regiment, 1814-1825.

2099. Trumpeter. L-Gds. Lancer Regiment, 1817-1818.

2100. Privates. Tsarevich Constantine Pavlovich's L.-Gds Lancer Regiment, 1818-1822.

2101. Non-Commissioned Officers. Tsarevich Constantine Pavlovich's L.-Gds Lancer Regiment, 1818-1822.

2102. Staff-Trumpeter and Trumpeter. Tsarevich Constantine Pavlovich's L.-Gds Lancer Regiment, 1818-1822.

2103. Field-Grade Officers. Tsarevich Constantine Pavlovich's L.-Gds Lancer Regiment, 1818-1822.

2104. Private and Non-Commissioned Officer. L.-Gds Lancer Regiment, 1818-1819.

2105. Field and Company-Grade Officers. L.-Gds Lancer Regiment, 1818-1819.

2106. NCO and Company-Grade Officer. Tsarevich Constantine Pavlovich's L.-Gds Lancer Regiment, 1819-1822.

2107. Trumpeters. Tsarevich Constantine Pavlovich's L.-Gds Lancer Regiment, 1825.

2108. Field-Grade Officers. Tsarevich Constantine Pavlovich's L.-Gds Lancer Regiment, 1825.

2109. Private and Non-Commissioned Officer. L.-Gds. Cossack Regiment, 1801-1809.

2110. Company-Grade Officers. L.-Gds Cossack Regiment, 1801-1809.

2111. Officer's cartridge pouch for the L.-Gds. Cossack Regiment, 1801-1808.

2112. Privates. L.-Gds Cossack Regiment, 1809-1812.

2113. Non-Commissioned Officers. L.-Gds Cossack Regiment, 1809-1812.

2114. Trumpeters. L.-Gds Cossack Regiment, 1809-1812.

2115. Company-Grade Officer and Field-Grade Officer. L.-Gds Cossack Regiment, 1809-1812.

2116. Officer's cartridge pouch for the L.-Gds. Cossack Regiment, instituted in 1809.

2117. General. L.-Gds Cossack Regiment, 1809-1812.

2118. Private and Non-Commissioned Officer. L.-Gds Cossack Regiment, 1812-1814.

2119. Company-Grade Officers. L.-Gds Cossack Regiment, 1812-1815.

2120. Privates. L.-Gds. Black Sea Squadron, 1815-1816.

2121. Non-Commissioned Officer. L.-Gds. Black Sea Squadron, 1813-1816.

2122. Privates. L.-Gds. Black Sea Squadron, 1816-1824. **Note**. *From 1817 gloves were without gauntlet cuffs.*

2123. Trumpeter. L.-Gds. Black Sea Squadron, 1816-1819.

2124. Company-Grade Officers. L.-Gds Cossack Regiment and L.-Gds. Black Sea Squadron, 1816-1819.

2125. Non-Commissioned Officer and Private. L.-Gds Cossack Regiment, 1816-1824.

2126. NCO of the L.-Gds Cossack Regiment, and Company-Grade Officer of the L.-Gds. Black Sea Squadron, 1819-1825.

2127. Trumpeters. L.-Gds Cossack Regiment and L.-Gds. Black Sea Squadron, 1820-1825.

2128. Private and Non-Commissioned Officer. L.-Gds. Black Sea Squadron, 1825.

2129. Field-Grade Officer. L.-Gds Cossack Regiment, 1825.

2130. Non-Commissioned Officer and Private. L.-Gds. Gendarme Half-Squadron, 1815-1816.

2131. Company-Grade Officers. L.-Gds Gendarme Half-Squadron, 1815-1816.

2132. Embroidery on Officers' coats in the L.-Gds. Gendarme Half-Squadron, established in 1815.

2133. Trumpeter and Company-Grade Officer. L.-Gds Gendarme Half-Squadron, 1816-1817.

2134. Company-Grade Officer. L.-Gds Gendarme Half-Squadron, 1817-1825.

2135. Trumpeter. L.-Gds Gendarme Half-Squadron, 1820-1825.

2136. Private and Non-Commissioned Officer. Guards Train Brigade, 1817-1825.

2137. Company-Grade Officer. Guards Train Brigade, 1817-1825.

Private. L.-Gds. Hussar Regiment, 1801-1802.

Company-Grade Officer. L.-Gds. Hussar Regiment, 1801-1802

Company-Grade Officer. L.-Gds. Hussar Regiment, 1801-1802. (In full parade uniform.)

Privates. L.-Gds. Hussar Regiment, 1801-1809

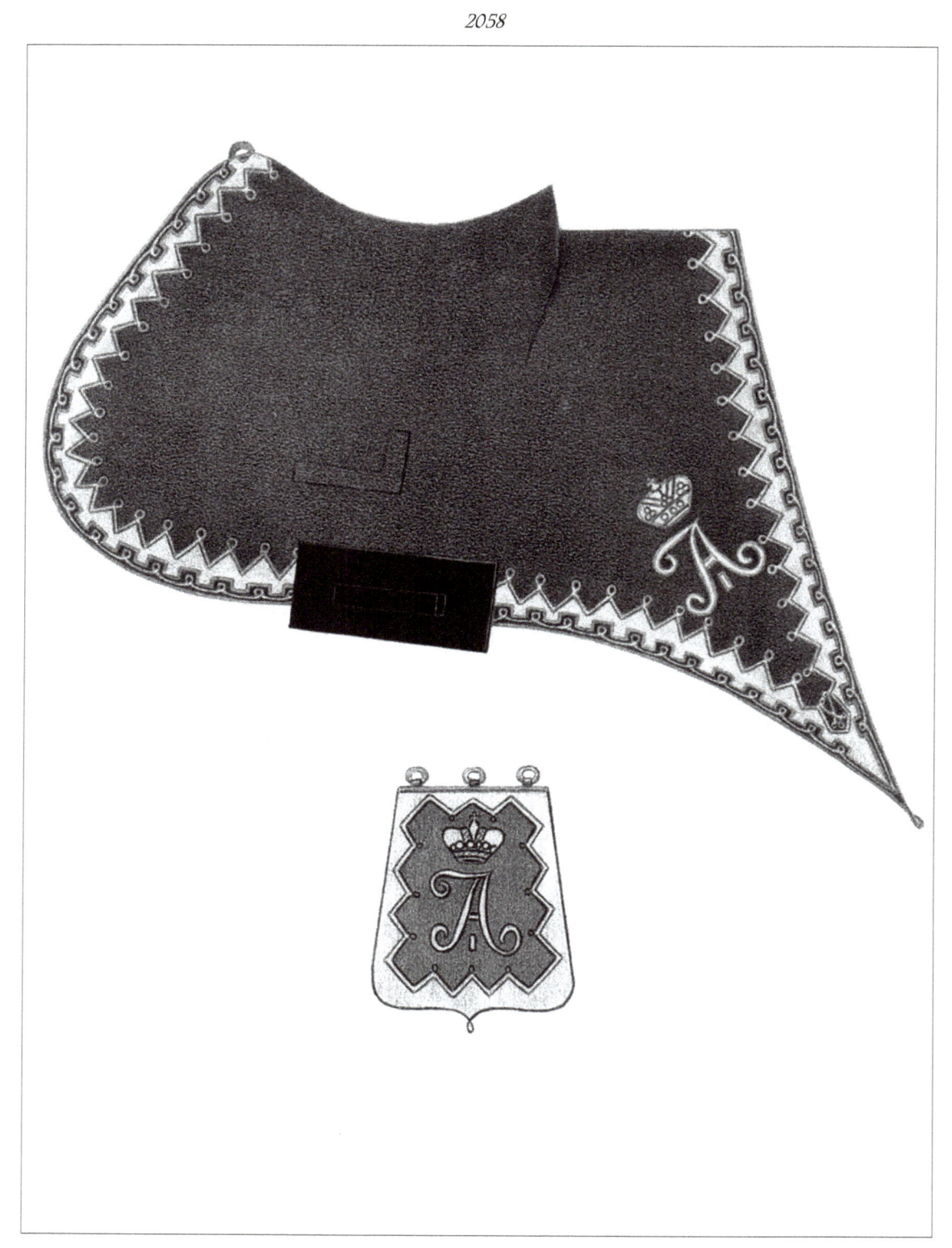

Saddlecloth and Sabertache for lower ranks in the L.-Gds. Hussar Regiment, since 1802.

Non-Commissioned Officer. L.-Gds. Hussar Regiment, 1802-180

Staff-Trumpeter and Trumpeter. L.-Gds. Hussar Regiment, 1802-1807

Company-Grade Officer. L.-Gds. Hussar Regiment, 1802-1809

Officer's sabertache, L.-Gds. Hussar Regiment, established in 1802

Company-Grade Officer. L.-Gds. Hussar Regiment, 1802-1804

Field-Grade Officer. L.-Gds. Hussar Regiment, 1807-1809

Private. L.-Gds. Hussar Regiment, 1809-1810

Lace figure [tsyfrovka] on the chakchiry pants of lower ranks in the L.-Gds. Hussar Regiment, established in 1809

Company-Grade Officers. L.-Gds. Hussar Regiment, 1809-1810

Decoration and lace figure on Officers' chakchiry pants in the L.-Gds. Hussar Regiment, 1809-1816

Company-Grade Officer. L.-Gds. Hussar Regiment, 1809

Private and Staff-Trumpeter. L.-Gds. Hussar Regiment, 1810-1811

Private and Staff-Trumpeter. L.-Gds. Hussar Regiment, 1812-1816

Company-Grade Officer. L.-Gds. Hussar Regiment, 1812-1816

Company-Grade Officers. L.-Gds. Hussar Regiment, 1814-1818

2074

Private. L.-Gds. Hussar Regiment, 1816-1819

Lace figure on the chakchiry pants of lower ranks in the L.-Gds. Hussar Regiment, established in 1816

Company-Grade Officer. L.-Gds. Hussar Regiment, 1816-1819

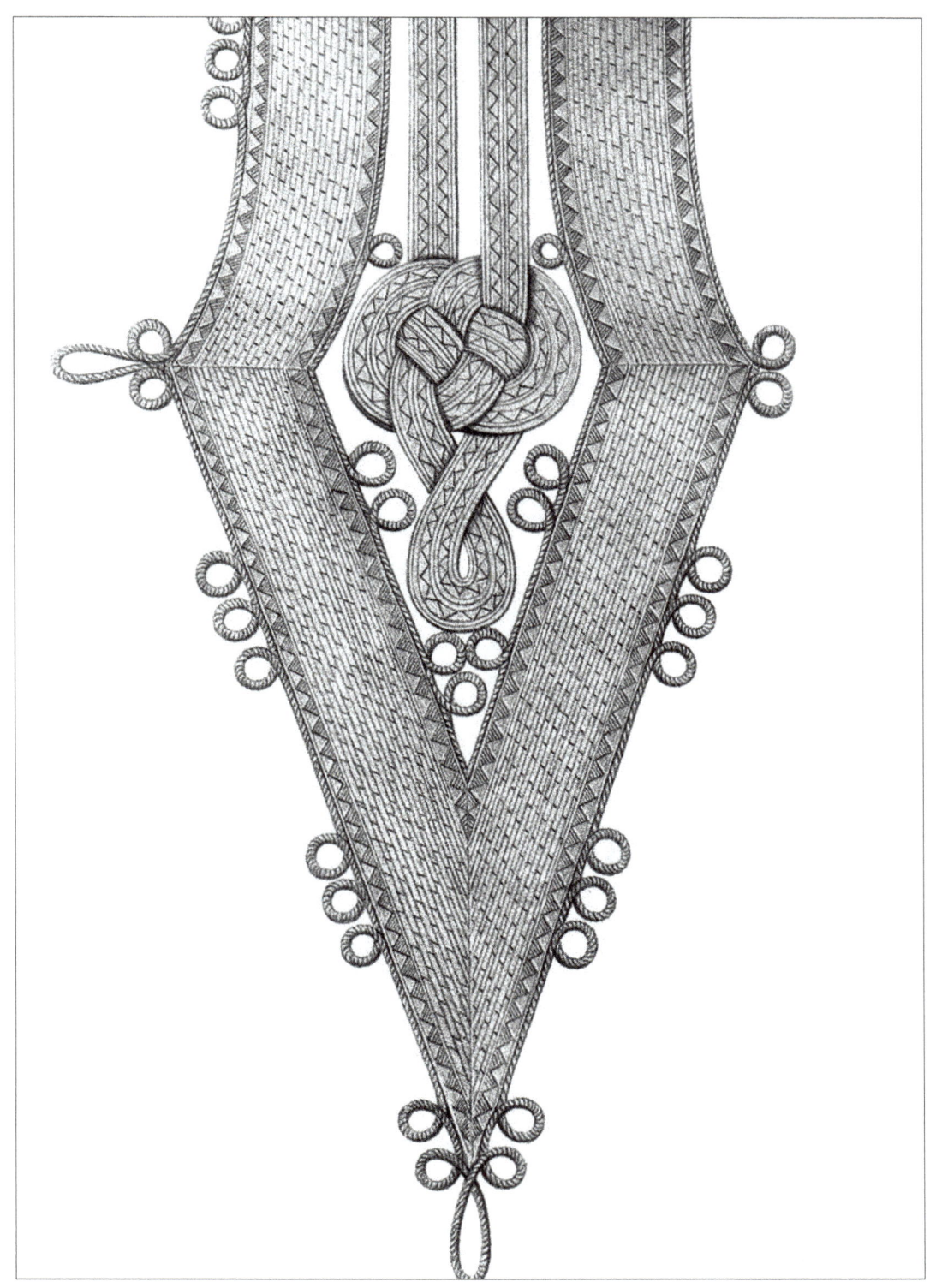

Decoration and lace figure on Officers' chakchiry pants in the L.-Gds. Hussar Regiment, established in 1816

Private and Trumpeter. L.-Gds. Hussar Regiment, 1817-1819

Embroidery on undress coat, L.-Gds. Hussar Regiment, since 1818

Private and Company-Grade Officer. L.-Gds. Hussar Regiment, 1819-1820

Company-Grade Officer and Non-Commissioned Officer. L.-Gds. Hussar Regiment, 1823-1825

Private. L.-Gds Hussar Regiment, 1824-1825

Shako for lower ranks of the L.-Gds. Hussar Regiment, 1824-1825

Shako for lower ranks of the L.-Gds. Grodno Hussar Regiment, 1824-1825. Note. This shako was prescribed for use, but was never used in the regiment.

Saddle cloths for lower ranks of the L.-Gds. Grodno Hussar Regiment, 1824-1825. a. Prescribed for use. b. Actually used

Company-Grade Officer. L.-Gds. Grodno Hussar Regiment, 1824-1825

Officers' shakos of the L.-Gds. Grodno Hussar Regiment, 1824-1825. a.a. Prescribed for Company-Grade Officers, but was not used. b.b.
Prescribed for Field-Grade Officers, but was not used. c.c. Actually used by Field and Company-Grade Officers

Officer's saddle cloth and sabertache of the L.-Gds. Grodno Hussar Regiment, 1824-1825

Field-Grade Officer. L.-Gds. Grodno Hussar Regiment, 1824-1825

Privates. L.-Gds. Lancer Regiment, 1809-1811

Non-Commissioned Officer. L.-Gds. Lancer Regiment, 1809-1811

Trumpeter and Staff-Trumpeter. L.-Gds. Lancer Regiment, 1809-1811

Company-Grade Officers. L.-Gds. Lancer Regiment, 1809-1811

Field-Grade Officer. L.-Gds. Lancer Regiment, 1807-1811

Staff-Trumpeter and Private. L.-Gds. Lancer Regiment, 1812-1814

Company-Grade Officer. L.-Gds. Lancer Regiment, 1814-1818

Non-Commissioned Officer and Private. L.-Gds. Lancer Regiment, 1814-1825

Trumpeter. L-Gds. Lancer Regiment, 1817-1818

Privates. Tsarevich Constantine Pavlovich's L.-Gds Lancer Regiment, 1818-1822

Non-Commissioned Officers. Tsarevich Constantine Pavlovich's L.-Gds Lancer Regiment, 1818-1822

Staff-Trumpeter and Trumpeter. Tsarevich Constantine Pavlovich's L.-Gds Lancer Regiment, 1818-1822

Field-Grade Officers. Tsarevich Constantine Pavlovich's L.-Gds Lancer Regiment, 1818-1822

Private and Non-Commissioned Officer. L.-Gds Lancer Regiment, 1818-1819

Field and Company-Grade Officers. L.-Gds Lancer Regiment, 1818-1819

Non-Commissioned Officer and Company-Grade Officer. Tsarevich Constantine Pavlovich's L.-Gds Lancer Regiment, 1819-1822

Trumpeters. Tsarevich Constantine Pavlovich's L.-Gds Lancer Regiment, 1825

Field-Grade Officers. Tsarevich Constantine Pavlovich's L.-Gds Lancer Regiment, 1825

Private and Non-Commissioned Officer. L.-Gds. Cossack Regiment, 1801-1809

Company-Grade Officers. L.-Gds Cossack Regiment, 1801-1809

Officer's cartridge pouch for the L.-Gds. Cossack Regiment, 1801-1808 - Officer's cartridge pouch for the L.-Gds. Cossack Regiment, instituted in 1809

Privates. L.-Gds Cossack Regiment, 1809-1812

Non-Commissioned Officers. L.-Gds Cossack Regiment, 1809-1812

Trumpeters. L.-Gds Cossack Regiment, 1809-1812

Company-Grade Officer and Field-Grade Officer. L.-Gds Cossack Regiment, 1809-1812

General. L.-Gds Cossack Regiment, 1809-1812

Private and Non-Commissioned Officer. L.-Gds Cossack Regiment, 1812-1814

Company-Grade Officers. L.-Gds Cossack Regiment, 1812-1815

Privates. L.-Gds. Black Sea Squadron, 1815-1816

Non-Commissioned Officer. L.-Gds. Black Sea Squadron, 1813-1816

Privates. L.-Gds. Black Sea Squadron, 1816-1824. Note. From 1817 gloves were without gauntlet cuffs

Trumpeter. L.-Gds. Black Sea Squadron, 1816-1819

Company-Grade Officers. L.-Gds Cossack Regiment and L.-Gds. Black Sea Squadron, 1816-1819

Non-Commissioned Officer and Private. L.-Gds Cossack Regiment, 1816-1824

Non-Commissioned Officer of the L.-Gds Cossack Regiment, and Company-Grade Officer of the L.-Gds. Black Sea Squadron, 1819-1825

Trumpeters. L.-Gds Cossack Regiment and L.-Gds. Black Sea Squadron, 1820-1825

Private and Non-Commissioned Officer. L.-Gds. Black Sea Squadron, 1825

Field-Grade Officer. L.-Gds Cossack Regiment, 1825

Non-Commissioned Officer and Private. L.-Gds. Gendarme Half-Squadron, 1815-1816

Company-Grade Officers. L.-Gds Gendarme Half-Squadron, 1815-1816

Embroidery on Officers' coats in the L.-Gds. Gendarme Half-Squadron, established in 1815

Trumpeter and Company-Grade Officer. L.-Gds Gendarme Half-Squadron, 1816-1817

Company-Grade Officer. L.-Gds Gendarme Half-Squadron, 1817-1825

Trumpeter. L.-Gds Gendarme Half-Squadron, 1820-1825

Private and Non-Commissioned Officer. Guards Train Brigade, 1817-1825

Company-Grade Officer. Guards Train Brigade, 1817-1825

SOLDIERS, WEAPONS & UNIFORMS ALREADY PUBLISHED
(SOME TITLES)

UNIFORMS OF RUSSIAN ARMY IN THE ERA OF ANCIENT TZAR
FROM THE REIGN OF VASILI IV TO MICHAEL I, ALEXIS, FEODOR III DURING THE XVII th CENTURY
A.V.VISKOVATOV — LUCA STEFANO CRISTINI
SWU-600-004

UNIFORMS OF RUSSIAN ARMY OF PETER I THE GREAT
FROM THE REIGN OF PETER I TO CATHERINE I, PEER II, ANNA AND IVAN VI, 1682-1741
A.V.VISKOVATOV — LUCA STEFANO CRISTINI
SWU-700-006

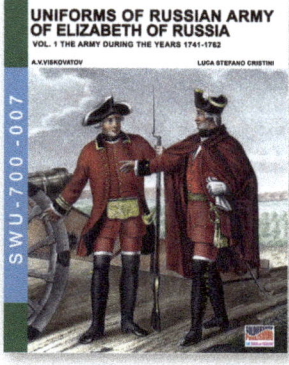

UNIFORMS OF RUSSIAN ARMY OF ELIZABETH OF RUSSIA
VOL. 1 THE ARMY DURING THE YEARS 1741-1762
A.V.VISKOVATOV — LUCA STEFANO CRISTINI
SWU-700-007

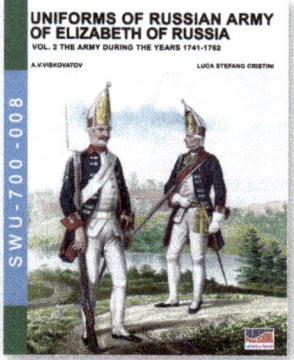

UNIFORMS OF RUSSIAN ARMY OF ELIZABETH OF RUSSIA
VOL. 2 THE ARMY DURING THE YEARS 1741-1762
A.V.VISKOVATOV — LUCA STEFANO CRISTINI
SWU-700-008

UNIFORMS OF RUSSIAN ARMY IN THE XVIII CENTURY VOL. 1
UNDER THE REIGN OF CATHERINE II EMPRESS OF RUSSIA BETWEEN 1762 AND 1796
A.V.VISKOVATOV — LUCA STEFANO CRISTINI
SWU-700-005

UNIFORMS OF RUSSIAN ARMY IN THE XVIII CENTURY VOL. 2
UNDER THE REIGN OF CATHERINE II EMPRESS OF RUSSIA BETWEEN 1762 AND 1796
A.V.VISKOVATOV — LUCA STEFANO CRISTINI
SWU-700-009

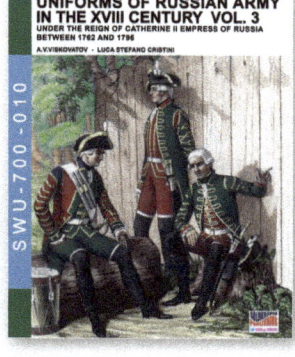

UNIFORMS OF RUSSIAN ARMY IN THE XVIII CENTURY VOL. 3
UNDER THE REIGN OF CATHERINE II EMPRESS OF RUSSIA BETWEEN 1762 AND 1796
A.V.VISKOVATOV — LUCA STEFANO CRISTINI
SWU-700-010

UNIFORMS OF RUSSIAN ARMY IN THE XVIII CENTURY VOL. 4
UNDER THE REIGN OF CATHERINE II EMPRESS OF RUSSIA BETWEEN 1762 AND 1796
A.V.VISKOVATOV — LUCA STEFANO CRISTINI
SWU-700-011

BRITISH ARMY UNIFORMS IN 1742
IN THE ART OF JOHN PINE
SWU-700-001

PRUSSIAN & AUSTRIAN ARMY UNIFORMS IN 1742-1770
LUCA STEFANO CRISTINI
SWU-700-002

THE FRENCH ARMY OF ANCIEN RÉGIME Volume 1
IN THE ART OF FELIX PHILIPPOTEAUX
LUCA STEFANO CRISTINI
SWU-700-003

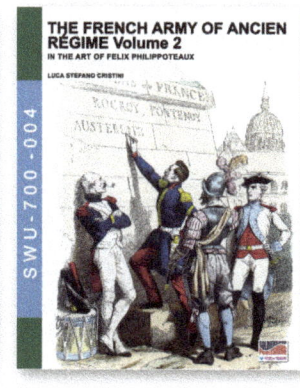

THE FRENCH ARMY OF ANCIEN RÉGIME Volume 2
IN THE ART OF FELIX PHILIPPOTEAUX
LUCA STEFANO CRISTINI
SWU-700-004

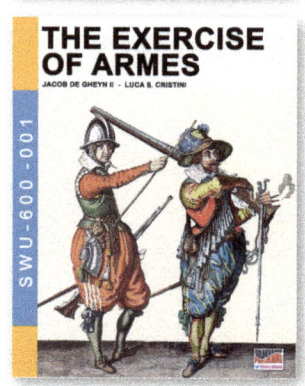

THE EXERCISE OF ARMES
JACOB DE GHEYN II — LUCA S. CRISTINI
SWU-600-001

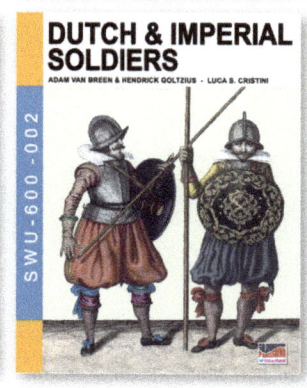

DUTCH & IMPERIAL SOLDIERS
ADAM VAN BREEN & HENDRICK GOLTZIUS — LUCA S. CRISTINI
SWU-600-002

HORSEMEN IN THE 16TH & 17TH C.
JACOB DE GHEYN II — A.DE BRUYN — LUCA S. CRISTINI
SWU-600-003

IMPERIAL SOLDIERS & UNIFORMS 1640-1860
IN THE ART OF FRANZ GERASCH
LUCA S.CRISTINI — Plates by FRANZ GERASCH
SWU-GEN-001